how to
love your
kids
more than
you hate
your ex

helen fried

hatherleigh

Hatherleigh Press is committed to preserving and protecting the natural resources of the earth. Environmentally responsible and sustainable practices are embraced within the company's mission statement.

Visit us at www.hatherleighpress.com and register online for free offers, discounts, special events, and more.

How to Love Your Kids More Than You Hate Your Ex
Text copyright © 2014 Helen Fried

Library of Congress Cataloging-in-Publication Data is available upon request.
ISBN: 978-1-57826-516-9

Cover and Interior Design by Carolyn Kasper

Printed in the United States
10 9 8 7 6 5 4 3 2 1

CONTENTS

....

Introduction 1

Why Me? 3

I HATE THAT #@%$&! 17

What Is Child Support for Anyway? 29

The "Cat's in the Cradle" Syndrome 41

He Said, She Said 51

Never Forget, YOU Are the Parent 61

Who Invited HER/HIM? 77

BOUNDARIES! 87

Teens Cry, Too 99

You Can't Un-ring a Bell 107

Would You Rather Be Happy or Right? 115

Final Word 123

INTRODUCTION

....

Hello friends,

    If you have this book in your hands, you are most likely a parent and are either divorced or are in the process of a divorce.

Your anxiety at the prospect of raising children in the midst of this major life change can be daunting. Your feelings of loss, anger, and helplessness can be overwhelmingly painful and confusing—not just for you, but for your children as well. Learning how to acknowledge, accept, and embrace change will be pivotal on your road to personal healing and successful co-parenting.

How to Love Your Kids More Than You Hate Your Ex is a short, easy and uplifting read that will help you move forward through this difficult time in your life. Providing positive suggestions, helpful ideas, motivational quotes, and insightful poems, this book aims to help you to stay focused and positive on what's important: *your children.*

Above all else, remember to LOVE your kids more than you HATE your ex!

Stop right there! There will be *no* "why me's" allowed here. It's unfortunate, but the "happily ever after" you envisioned for yourself with your ex is no more. One or both of you has moved on from the marriage; whether it was emotionally, spiritually, or physically, the marriage has run its course. Wasting your energy and time on asking, "Why me?" will benefit no one.

I'm not saying it will be easy. What I *am* saying is that you need to remember that you have children who are looking to you for strength and guidance. This is not the time to wallow, crumble, or falter; this is the time to find your inner strength and press on.

So, first things first: Stop looking at the wedding video. In fact, push "eject" and take that DVD out of the machine! Put away all the old photo albums. Stop dreaming about what *could* have been and start planning on what *will* be. This is the time to dust off your knees, stand tall, and begin moving forward. Remember—you are not on this journey alone. You have beautiful children who are going to need you now more than ever. It's time to take stock of everything and keep keeping on!

Keep Busy

Now is the perfect time to accept those dinner invitations offered by friends and family. It's time to go to that art exhibit, or that concert in the park you've been wanting to see. It's time to pick up that book you've been meaning to read, or join that mommy/daddy group you saw advertised in your local paper. The benefit to keeping busy is it helps your mind to stop swirling and twirling in the abyss of answerless questions.

Keep Calm and Keep *Busy*!

. . . .

*"Inaction breeds doubt and
fear. Action breeds confidence and courage. If you
want to conquer fear, do not
sit home and think about it.
Go out and get busy."*

—DALE CARNEGIE

. . . .

Stay Healthy

Staying healthy at this time will not only
benefit you, it will also benefit your child.
A healthy body is the first step to a healthy
mind. So get up off the couch, sign up for
that 6:00 P.M. yoga class or that Saturday

afternoon spin class, and then *go*. If you're not the gym type, a walk or bike ride can be just as rewarding, as well as a great opportunity to spend some quality time with your child. Finding healthy, yummy recipes is as easy as a click on the Internet. This is your time to take back control of your mind, body, and soul.

. . . .

"To keep the body in good health is a duty...otherwise we shall not be able to keep our mind strong and clear."

—BUDDHA

. . . .

Find Support

Chances are, you are *not* the only person in your circle of friends or coworkers who has traveled the road of divorce. Within them, you may find a comforting word or an inspiring similarity to your own journey. They may have a great list of "do's and don'ts" that you can benefit positively from. They can be great sounding boards at a time when you feel that no one understands.

However, some of us may not feel comfortable expressing ourselves to someone so familiar. This is when finding a good therapist can be helpful. Don't be too proud to seek support. Your happiness, sanity and your child's well-being are non-negotiable.

It's important to actively protect yourself and your children from the potentially damaging after-shocks of divorce. Your goal should be to get your spirit emotionally healthy and your mind mentally strong. That's what *you* need right now, and it's what your children need from you.

. . . .

"It takes a great man to give sound advice tactfully, but a greater to accept it graciously."

—Logan P. Smith

. . . .

Your Inner Strength

Your children are just as frightened, confused, angry, and disappointed as you are. They have just had their world turned upside down, too. The fear of the unknown can be quite overwhelming for their minds to wrap themselves around. You might not have all the answers right now—no, wait; you *definitely* won't have all the answers right now—but this is the time for you to "fake it 'til you make it." When they look for you to be their safe place, you need to look back with confidence in your eyes and harmony in your heart. Find your inner strength and be the parent they need you to be.

. . . .

"Out of suffering have
emerged the strongest souls;
the most massive characters
are seared with scars."

—KHALIL GIBRAN

. . . .

Set Goals

Setting goals should be a constant in both yours and your children's lives. To begin, start by writing down where you want to see yourself in a week, a month, six months, a year. Setting goals will help you create a positive outline of which direction you choose for your life to go. Although there might be one less number in the equation, it should not hinder the sum of your life.

Setting Goals 101:

Start small. Make your early goals simple and easily attainable. At the outset, it's important to give you and your children the confidence to continue progressing at this uncertain time in your lives. Begin with one-week goals; for your children, something as basic as *learning to tie their shoes, make their bed every day, read a book a night/week, take* *out trash*, etc.; for you, try things like *learn a new recipe, start a work-out regimen, read a book, clean out a closet*, etc. Eventually, you and your children will be able to move on to more challenging, long-term goals. Examples include *improving math grades* or *learning a new language* for your kids, and *save for a vacation or new car* or *go back to school* for you. No goal is too small or too big—just pace yourself!

Be a role model. Lead by example; make your goals known to your children, and keep the dialogue open to discuss progress and set-backs. Make this a positive learning experience for all of you.

Keep positive. Never miss an opportunity to let your children know when they are doing well. Praise their progress and positively promote their goals. Once a goal is complete, take time to celebrate your successes! Steer away from store-bought rewards; make it more personal whenever possible. Give your children several healthy options (a quality-time picnic, a day at the beach/park, a special dinner, family bowling night, horseback riding) and then let them choose how they would like to celebrate their accomplishments.

. . . .

"What you get by achieving your goals is not as important as what you become by achieving your goals."

—Zig Ziglar

. . . .

WHY ME?

Why me?
How quickly I was set free.
I tried to hold on so tight,
only to lose this painful fight.
Why was my love unable to prevail?
I never expected my "I do's" to fail.
I don't understand
Where did it all go so wrong
Am I capable of standing strong?
I battle to feel less broken;
to refrain from the love I've unspoken.
I must search, deep in my soul
There I will find the light
to keep my mind whole in this dark fight.

I am blessed with a child
who looks for guidance in my eyes
it is my job to look back
for him to see strength and sanity
Even if they should be lies.

I HATE THAT #@%$&!

Chances are there will come a time when these words will depart your lips:

"I *HATE* THAT #@%$&!"

Don't worry; you're not alone.

You might be wondering how it is possible to despise someone you once walked down the aisle with; the person to whom you professed your undying love. Well, wonder no more: anger is an inevitable emotion that will occasionally rear its ugly head. There are very few people who can get you as angry as your ex. After all, they know the secret buttons to push and the locations of all your hidden Achilles' heels. So be prepared: There *will* be some hitting below the belt, and you run the risk of having the wind knocked out of you.

You may also be feeling anger toward your ex because you perceive them as the initiator of the divorce. You may feel that they single-handedly destroyed your world; that, if it wasn't for them, your life would still be perfect. Let's inject a dose of reality into that thought: NOT TRUE. Your life would not be perfect. Your ex left you because the relationship was *broken*; because your love alone could not sustain the marriage.

Yes, it is a harsh reality. But you will need to be honest with yourself in order to move forward. With anger, a parent is prone to making irrational decisions, thinking they are punishing their ex. But in reality, you're just as likely to be punishing your children. Don't make this about you and your ex; make it about you and your children.

You may never get to a place of amicability with your ex. As sad as that sounds, it runs very true for many. You have no control over how they think or how they choose to behave. You must choose to be the hero in this story and never forget to LOVE your kids more than you HATE your ex!

Top 5 Do-*Not*-Do's

Do Not: *Hinder your child from receiving a phone call from your ex.*

Allowing your child to openly communicate with their parent will give them a sense of calm in the storm. Just because, for you, your ex-spouse's voice is like nails running down a chalk board, this does not mean that holds true for your child. It is important for them to try to keep some sense of normalcy during this unstable time in their lives. Sometimes, just the sound of the other parent's voice is enough to bring some peace in an uncertain situation.

Do Not: *Bad mouth your ex in front of your children.*

They hear you! I don't care how quietly you *think* you speak, whisper, or spell. They hear you! Their little antennas are up and out and they are honing in on every syllable spoken. With that, they will interpret every negative word as something that they caused. Allow them to live in innocence for as long as possible. This will be one of the greatest gifts you can give them.

Do Not: *Financially withhold from your child.* Sadly, this one happens way too often. Many times, the only power and control an ex feels they have left is that of monetary means. Don't punish your child this way. If you can afford it, do it.

Do Not: *Miss promised visitation.* Your child will have many disappointments in their life. Don't make one of them your constantly giving them empty promises.

Do Not: *Withhold important information regarding your child from your ex.*

Try to refrain from cop-outs like, "Oh, you never asked" or, "If the children were important to you, you would *know* their school/athletic schedule." Stop being petty. It doesn't take much energy to send a text or shoot an email to keep your ex informed. Above all, don't punish your child for your ex's shortcomings.

Which Way to the High Road?

When planning your journey through divorce, making the correct turn onto the High Road is key to charting the route you'll want to take. Don't get distracted by Aggravation Avenue or Hothead Highway. Stay focused, and stay on course. I know that, at times, you may have an overwhelming desire to go off-roading (maybe do a few wheelies) at your ex's expense, but please—stay on track. Staying focused taking the High Road will

make both you and your children powerful
and proud.

· ·

> *"He who controls others may*
> *be powerful, but he who has*
> *mastered himself is might-*
> *ier still."*
>
> —LAO TZU

· ·

Choose the Right Time to Talk

You don't need to be a rocket scientist to
know that initiating a conversation with
your ex while tensions are running high is
a bad move. No productive or constructive

dialogue will be possible at this time. Your best bet is to write down the issues you wish to discuss and your personal concerns, and raise the matter at a later time. When tension levels have calmed a bit, then you can try to revisit your concerns in a positive and mature setting.

What you might also find helpful is to create a "code word." A code word is a word or phrase that you and your ex can agree upon and use for adult "time out" situations.

Example: Your conversation is getting heated, and one of you realizes that nothing good is going to come of it. That's when one of you blurts out the code word ("chocolate chip," "Chardonnay," "Yankees," etc.). Once the code word has been invoked, the conversation *must* cease until a later date. This gives both parties time to calm down; time to reflect and revisit the issue later. The key is to make the code word something neutral and somewhat silly; doing so will aid in calming a tense situation. This works almost every time!

. . . .

"You win battles by knowing the enemy's timing, and using a timing which the enemy does not expect."

—MIYAMOTO MUSASHI

. . . .

I HATE...

I hate the way you make me feel

I hate that I just let you win

I hate the way my pain's so real

I hate the way my air's so thin

I hate how for you, it's no big deal

I hate that I can't stop the spin

I hate my heart that will not heal

I hate the punches to my chin

I hate the sadness I can't conceal

I hate the storm that blows within

I hate the way you make me feel

I hate that I just let you win

WHAT IS CHILD SUPPORT FOR ANYWAY?

According to the WordNet Dictionary, the definition of child support is as follows:

. . . .

Child Support, n. *Court-ordered support paid by one spouse to the other, who has custody of the children after the parents are separated.*

. . . .

Okay, so we have the "definition." That tells us what it *is;* but what is it *for?*

Child support is to be used for the child's basic necessities: food, clothing, and shelter. Obviously, children need nutritious food, proper clothing, and a safe and comfortable place to live. At a minimum, child support may be used to purchase groceries and appropriate clothing, and help to defray the child's related shelter costs, such as mortgage or rent and lighting, telephone, and utility bills.

Which expenses are *not* included in child support varies state by state. In general, extracurricular activities, such as summer camps, sports activities, uninsured medical expenses, and educational expenses are *not* included in the basic support amount, unless specifically included in the divorce settlement agreement.

It seems pretty clear-cut and practical, doesn't it? In theory, yes; but sadly, this is where a few of us get stuck. Paying your child support check on time every month is not the beginning and end of raising your child. There are many unforeseen expenses in raising a child, and it is your responsibility as a parent to make sure you provide for them the best life you can. Childhood, from 0–18 years old (6,574 days, but who's counting?) is the shortest period of time in a person's life. To spend that time—*their* time—nickel and diming over who's going to pay for Johnny's baseball or Mary's ballet is selfish and childish. The only ones who suffer in those scenarios are the children.

Bottom line: If you can afford it, do it! Stop playing the victim and remember to *love* your kids *more* than you hate your ex.

Plant Your Own Garden

If you are the recipient of child support, then hopefully your ex does right by you and never forgets the most important thing: that, above all else, it's about the children. But sadly, for some of us this can be an exhausting battle lasting 18 years, with heartbreaking consequences.

What you need to do is this: Plant your *own* garden. Stop waiting for someone else to bring you flowers. Be resourceful, be responsible, be proficient, and be prepared.

It's easy as A–B–C!

A: Accept and **A**cknowledge that downsizing may be in your future. Remember that you and your children are more valuable than the size of your house or the style of your car. Take pride in where you live regardless, and work hard to make your house a home. Your children will take pride in what they have if *you* do.

B: Budget, **B**udget, **B**udget. **B**e prepared—that rainy day *will* eventually come. If you are unable to depend on your ex for adequate child support, then *you* must be the hero. Budget and save; enjoy the sunshine as you prepare for the deluge.

C: **C**ut up those **C**redit **C**ards! It's time to make mature and responsible choices. Right now, cash is your friend and credit cards are your enemy. Until you are comfortable with your financial situation, refrain from the peril of escalating interest rates. So long as you avoid spending beyond your means, you'll be in a much better position moving forward.

. . . .

"In the long run, we shape our lives, and we shape ourselves. The process never ends until we die. And the choices we make are ultimately our own responsibility."

—ELEANOR ROOSEVELT

. . . .

Cohabitating

There comes a time when your ex enters into the next step in their new relationship (cohabitation), where many of us who are paying child support go into a downward spiral. You start having wild thoughts of your ex and their new partner, sitting around counting all their loot—*your* hard-earned money—and planning for their next European vacation. This can become especially difficult if your ex has moved on first; it may be that you are allowing your pain and insecurity to negatively affect your actions. You must choose to be bigger than your jealousy and remember it's not about your ex; it's about the happiness, success and well-being of your children.

Others take the exact opposite approach: You may feel that, now that your ex is back in a dual-income household, your funds are now less important. You may feel that it is time for someone else to pick up the slack. But as much as you may wish this to be a reality, it couldn't be further from the truth. Your children are still *your* children; they are not the responsibility of your ex's new partner. Look at your monthly payments not as a gift to your ex, but as you doing right by your kids. Your objective should be to offer your children the best childhood possible, filled with joyful memories. The bottom line remains: If you can afford it, DO IT!

. . . .

"That old law about 'an eye for an eye' leaves everybody blind. The time is always right to do the right thing."

—MARTIN LUTHER KING, JR.

. . . .

Root of All Evil

Since the beginning of time, money has been synonymous with evil and greed. Your child shouldn't be made to feel the emotional burden of your divorce, and that goes double for the financial burden. For some of you, keeping a tight rein on your funds is the only sense of control and power you feel you have left in the relationship. Please stop this immediately—your children are more important than your money. Don't make the issue of money an unnecessary source of anxiety for your children. So remember: If you can afford to do something, do it. It presents another opportunity to appear confident and strong in front of your children, to let them know that everything's going to be okay.

. . . .

"For the love of money is the root of all evil: which while some coveted after, they have erred from faith, and pierced themselves through with many sorrows."

—TIMOTHY 6:10

. . . .

NICKEL AND DIME

Why do you Nickel and Dime?
Are your children not worth your time?
You feel you need to punish me.
But hating me won't set you free.

Your children should not suffer for the anger
    in your heart.
You know as well as I it's not their fault our
    love did part.

They're more than pawns in games of pain.
Don't limit what they can attain.
Is money all that you desire?
Should not our children value higher?

I hope that soon you'll start to see
this money's not for you or me.
When you withhold your promised sum,
I'm not the one you're stealing from.

THE "CAT'S IN THE CRADLE" SYNDROME

....

Let me give you one simple tip to avoid a lot of headaches and heartbreaks: stop making promises you can't keep. If you tell your child you're planning on taking them to dinner, or that you'll be at their football game, or that you'll make time to watch the new routine they learned in gymnastics, you need to be there—come hell or high water. You need to make your child a *priority*, rather than an afterthought.

Divorcing your spouse does not mean divorcing your child. What it *does* mean is that, now more than ever, you need to make every effort to let them know that you still are, and will always be, a part of their life. This is not the time for abandonment or broken promises; this is the time to own up to the responsibility of being a parent—a parent your child can count on, believe in, and be proud of.

Yes, this might not always be convenient or easy. And yes, it might put a damper on your evening plans. But a few hours that you sacrifice for your child now will reward them with a lifetime of memories. Life is about making memories. Don't be absent from their mental scrapbook.

Make Time

No more excuses, no more broken promises, and no more maybes. We all work; we all have business dinners and important "can't miss" meetings. However, once you are divorced, the same rules do not apply; these are no longer acceptable excuses for not spending time with your child. There is no longer a dual parent household; your child looks forward to every scheduled visit. It makes them feel worthy, loved, and important. Don't make them look to strangers for the attention and social nourishment they so desire from you. Even something as simple as having dinner together once a week or paying a visit to the book store together will be priceless to them. Make time for your children...or before long, they won't want to make time for you.

. . . .

"At the end of the day, the most overwhelming key to a child's success is the positive involvement of parents."

—JANE D. HULL

. . . .

Be the Hero

Critical situations call out for a hero. So tie on your cape and tighten up your boot laces; you have it within you to be the hero your children need, and you are certainly needed! You know what has to be done. You need to stop looking over your shoulder to see what your ex is doing first; remember that this is not a competition, and that above all else you must put your children's well-being first. There are precious few years in your child's life (especially once they reach their teen years) where you will be considered a cool—or even an acceptable—presence to their friends. Relish the moments where you can swoop in and save the day! Be the hero!

. . . .

*"A hero is someone who
has given his or her life
to something bigger than
oneself."*

—JOSEPH CAMPBELL

. . . .

Make Memories

Time goes by so fast. Before you know it, you'll be seated in the stands at your child's high school graduation, proudly watching them as they walk down the aisle with a look of fulfillment and accomplishment on their face. They'll make their way boldly across the stage, firmly shake the hand of their school's dean and exit—as a brand-new young adult. And as they head back to their seat, walking a little bit taller than before, they will nervously turn to look for you.

Sadly, for many children the mental scrapbook they own has many missing pages of their parents. Fear of you being absent is a painful reality to them. You have the power to determine how your children think of you. Don't make their memories dwell on disappointments, uncertainty, angst, and anger.

Don't wait until it's too late to make memories with your children. Today, you cannot get back, and tomorrow may never come.

. . . .

"A life-long blessing for chil-
dren is to fill them with
warm memories of times
together. Happy memories
become treasures in the
heart to pull out on the
tough days of adulthood."

—CHARLOTTE DAVIS KASL

. . . .

CAT'S IN THE CRADLE

"Dinner next week, I'll make the time,
I'll be at your game, come rain or shine."
No more promises you can't keep
I'm tired of crying and losing sleep
I used to look for you in the stands
Rearranging all my plans
Why could you not make time for me?
I know now the parent I *will* not be.
I'm sorry if all of this hurts you to hear
Sometimes the truth hits the heart so near.
But I've cried the last tears that I plan
    to shed,
I'll spend no more nights crying in bed.

I must believe you know not what you do,
That you're blind to the pain that you put
    me through
So that even though you haven't a clue,
I'll never, ever stop loving you.

HE SAID,
SHE SAID

Your children do not need to visit the world of adulthood before their time. Your children are not your therapist, they are not your BFF, and they are not your sounding board. There is no need for them to listen to your belly-aching of how terrible their other parent is or how miserable your life is because of the divorce. You might feel that by informing your children of your ex's shortcomings it will somehow cast you in a brighter light. Well, think again. This will inevitably come back to bite you on the behind. Children are a lot smarter than we give them credit for. I promise you they will figure out on their own the shortcomings of both you and your ex, regardless of your dissertation.

In fact, the only thing that you will accomplish by bad mouthing your ex to your children is giving them an unnecessary education in the art of gossiping. If you set the ball rolling for them to view others and themselves negatively, they will learn to be bitter and angry. They will learn to doubt not only themselves, but you as well. So, when the urge comes over you to start venting your frustrations, make sure your audience is made up exclusively of your peers.

Let your children be children, let them worry about baby dolls, baseballs, and bubble gum...not court dates, conflict, credit cards, and new courtships. Please, *love* your kids more than you *hate* your ex.

Bite Your Tongue

It can be very tempting to speak ill of your ex. Many of us have some less-than flattering adjectives we like to use in describing our former partners, and it can be healthy to vent those feelings from time to time. The hope is that this too shall pass—over time. In the meantime, limit how often you let your ex's behavior "get to you." As satisfying as it can be in the short term to fly off the handle, it's better in the long term to keep calm, and carry on. Bite down on that tongue, put a smile on your face, and keep happy thoughts in your head! More than just for you, your children deserve to have mature adults as parents and role models. What they do *not* deserve is a pair of spoiled crybabies, who name-call and throw temper tantrums at the drop of a hat. Leave the childish shennanigans to the children; they're better at it, anyway.

• •

"The tongue like a sharp knife... It kills without drawing blood."

—BUDDHA

• •

Pick on Someone Your Own Age

It's tempting to fill the spaces your ex left behind with your children. But it's important to remember: whether you're single, divorced, or married, your children are *not* your friends—they're your *children*. Until you can share a beer or Chardonnay with them, they should remain your children and live as such. Too many parents (especially during a divorce) invite their children into the world of "grown-ups," way before the time is right. This is dangerous on several levels: A child's brain is not equipped to recognize adult issues and absorb them in a healthy manner.

In early childhood, the brain is developing the basics—gross motor skills of the legs, arms, and torso—followed by language and developing of social skills. Before you know it, they'll be in their adolesence; your teen might even be quite the social butterfly!

However, a crucial and very important part of their brain, called the frontal lobe, is not yet fully developed.

What is a frontal lobe, you ask? A frontal lobe is basically your child's "judgment button"; it's the, "Is this a good idea?" or, "What is the consequence of this action?" button. It's not that your teen doesn't have this button at all; they do. But their frontal lobe is still immature and a bit sluggish until early adulthood. Point being, they are not able to compartmentalize many of the adult situations you may feel the need to discuss with them.

Remember: Your children only have one childhood, so please allow them to enjoy it and grow into healthy, productive, and happy adults—in their own time. Save all your drama for someone your own age. Stop trying to make your children *like* you and just let them *love* you.

. . . .

"The well-being and welfare
of children should always
be our focus."

—TODD TIAHRT

. . . .

Take Control

You can't control what your ex says, and you can't control what your ex feels. But more than that, oftentimes you can't *know* these things, either. There will be times when you will be utterly dumbfounded and bewildered by the words and actions of your ex. You might find yourself looking around the room wondering where the hidden camera is!

Many of their tactics, motives, and outbursts will seem foolish, and may be motivated by anger and ignorance. You cannot predict how someone will process the experiece of divorce; people will surprise you, in both good and bad ways. Don't get tangled in a poisonous web of bitterness.

Take control of your emotions and think before you speak. Do not stoop down to the level of destructive words; no good ever comes of it. Remember to always take the high road. By choosing the high road, you give your child a lesson and a gift—the gift of patience, self control, class, and dignity.

. . . .

*"The most powerful weapon
is to not attack, but to be
able to have self-control."*

—DALAI LAMA

. . . .

PLEASE, I JUST WANT TO...

Please, I just want to go out and play and enjoy the sun on a beautiful day.

Please, I just want to be with my friends and not worry about what's happening back home.

Please, I just want to be silly and goofy and not need to worry that I'll make you angry.

Please, I just want to stay innocent and let my imagination run free and wild.

Please, I just want to lay down my head at night without hearing you fight.

Please, I just want to be a carefree kid; I don't need to know all the terrible things my other parent did.

Please.

NEVER FORGET, YOU ARE THE PARENT

....

n divorce, many parents have a hard time saying no, and struggle with setting con- structive boundaries for their children. By wavering on punishments or choosing to ignore and deny their poor behavior, you allow yourself to be their punching bag. This might be because you feel irrationally consumed with guilt, and are afraid of your children not liking you anymore.

Please, do not allow yourself to fall into this trap. It creates a cruel and detrimental display of poor parenting, at a time when your children will need your guidance more than ever before. During these times of stress and transition, a positive understanding of what is right and wrong is invaluable.

This is a time when many children will be testing waters and pushing limits. They may manipulate both you and your ex to see where the weakest link lies. So, even though you may have a plethora of emotions swarming through your mind, it's important to stand firm and stay consistent with your expectations from them.

The most prevalent emotion you will be feeling is probably guilt. So many flavors of guilt come with divorce: guilt of not being able to spend enough time with your child, guilt of being the initiator of the divorce, guilt of harboring ill feelings toward your ex; and these are just a few. Unfortunately, many believe that the remedy for their child's ill behavior is to allow them to run free, without consequences. However, taking this path of least resistance today will almost certainly guarantee the path of pain, disappointment, and heartache tomorrow.

You might want to begin by injecting the word "*no*" into your vocabulary. Start holding your children accountable for their actions. Losing key privileges or getting grounded because they failed to follow house rules will school them in one of life's greatest lessons. That being: Throughout life *you* and only *you* are responsible for and in control of your successes and failures.

And remember: little kids, little problems; big kids, big problems.

. . . .

> *"Our lives are a sum total of*
> *the choices we have made."*
> —WAYNE DYER

. . . .

Too Much Power

If *you* are the parent that gives or has given your child too much power, be prepared. Be *very* prepared, because you are in for a long and troublesome journey. Allowing a child to run the household as they see fit will inevitably destroy any sense of harmony in your life.

A child's mind, even an adolescent's, is not capable of compartmentalizing and orchestrating adult issues. All that will result is stress for you, and stress for your child. It's just that simple. Keep age-appropriate limitations on what they can control.

By not doing so, you run the very real risk of your child perceiving that they are the superior element in your home. They will begin believing that they "know best." Unfortunately, this is because you have allowed them too much power to make mature decisions and choices far before their time.

Their demeanor will begin to change; they will become more combative and angry. Believing themselves to be in charge of "addressing and fixing" the problems of the home, they'll grow more and more frustrated with each new conflict. They may look and act like they are in control and in charge, but don't be fooled. They are frightened, confused, and lonely, placed in an adult world where they have no business being.

If you're looking for the antidote, it's time to take a big swallow of the, "Oops, I was wrong" elixir. Your "power child" received their ailment from you; the parents. And it's *you*, the parents, who hold the cure. You need to begin by acknowledging and owning up to your faults. Let your child know that you were wrong in inviting and expecting them to take part in a world before they were ready.

It's time to keep mature conflicts and issues away from your "power child" and start replacing them with age-appropriate dilemmas for them to work on. Don't expect your "elixir" to be a miracle drug; the healing will be a long and slow process. However, if you and your ex stand united and consistent with your goals and expectations, your child's prognosis is excellent.

. . . .

*"An infallible way to make
your child fail is to satisfy
all his demands."*

—HENRY HOME

. . . .

Where Are My Manners?

Instilling manners is an extremely important part of raising a child. Manners are in
place to teach children how to be respectful
of others, their surroundings and, most
importantly, themselves. Without manners,
children learn rather to be entitled, rude,
unruly, and disrespectful. Don't rely on society or strangers to school your children in
manners; it is *your* responsibility as a parent
to teach your children right from wrong.

Do not be half-hearted or thoughtless;

your children deserve *all* the necessary tools to prepare them to become positive, polite, and productive members of society.

. . . .

> *"A man's manners are a*
> *mirror in which he shows*
> *his portrait."*
>
> —Johann Wolfgang
> von Goethe

. . . .

Consistency Is Key

Being consistent with your praise or punishments will allow your child to live without confusing maybes and "what ifs." Always say what you mean and mean what you say; children will learn quickly what is expected of them. No matter how difficult or how trying, you must not waiver on being the parent. You must stand firm on decisions made and carry them out. Your children are desperately looking for structure and stability in your actions, especially in the midst of a divorce. Be their rock and their voice of wisdom.

Consistency from both homes is essential. Many times, a parent has trouble "staying with the program," which leads to setbacks in your children's positive growth. Remember, children will look to the "weakest link" when trying to stretch the boundaries of acceptable conduct. We must recognize when we are guilty of failing to measure up to our own standards on the consistency front.

If you and your ex are having trouble being consistent and standing firm with your children, you may be caught up in one of the following unhealthy scenarios:

Good Cop: You're out to win the *"kids like me better"* trophy; instituting consistency with your children and in your home will not exist as long as that trophy remains on your mantel.

Anything-But-Bad Cop: You feel that the time you have with your children is limited and you reject setting up any consistent structure for fear it will paint you as the *"meanie."*

Good-Time Cop: You are too busy running off, looking for your next entertaining escapade, to keep any kind of consistency or structure within your home; keeping things consistent and together will be virtually impossible for you to execute until you begin viewing your responsibilities with the seriousness they deserve.

Do any of these scenarios sound familiar? Are you guilty of one, two or all three? If you said yes, then believe it or not, you are already one step closer to repairing your relationship with your children and succeeding on your journey to happy and healthy parenting. How? *You* just owned up to and acknowledged your mistakes; now realize that *you* alone have the power to change them.

It's time to begin revising your thinking and begin repairing the damage.

. . . .

"Our children are counting on us to provide two things: consistency and structure. Children need parents who say what they mean, mean what they say, and do what they say they are going to do."

—BARBARA COLOROSO

. . . .

R-E-S-P-E-C-T:
Find Out What It Means to *You*

Respect of others means accepting people as they are and valuing their point of view, even if it differs from your own. It means being open, and acknowledging when you're wrong. It means not dismissing people because they're different from you. It means giving respect where you wish to receive respect. It means being polite and kind; being kind to people should not be negotiable—and that includes your ex! Remember that your children will be looking to you as a model for how they will look at and deal with the world. When you practice being respectful to others you allow yourself and your children the opportunity to practice compassion and patience.

Self-respect means not allowing others to treat you badly. It means not falling prey to peer pressure, or trying to be someone you're not comfortable being. It's important to stay committed to your own self; never compromise on what you believe to be right. It means steering clear of jealousy, as being jealous of other's achievements and happiness will only inhibit your own path to success. Try being happy through others' successes, and realize that another's accomplishment in no way diminishes your own self-worth. The importance of teaching *and* learning self-respect will grant you and your children the confidence to be powerful and proud. You and *only* you are able to set the standard for how you are to be treated.

Respect of self and others both are essential for a happy, peaceful and prosperous existence. Stop looking to others for approval and start looking within yourself for your own greatness.

• •

"Respect for ourselves guides
our morals; respect for
others guides our manners."
                    —LAURENCE STERNE

• •

BECAUSE I SAID SO

"No, you may not's and Yes, you may go's

My words pull you confusingly, to and fro

I do this not because I wish you strife

I do this because it's all part of life

It's my job to set the limits and rules

And I know as my child you see this as cruel

But my only desire, in this world so vast

Is that you smile, succeed, and have a blast.

WHO INVITED HER/HIM?

If you're asking this question, chances are it's because your ex has a new squeeze. This can be a very difficult time for everyone—you, your children, even your circle of friends. You may be feeling a bit hurt that you were "replaced" or jealous that your ex has moved on without you. The reality has hit that reconciliation is not an option. And your child may be feeling much the same way; their fleeting hope of mommy and daddy getting back together has been crushed.

So, how do we handle this one? The simple answer is—with dignity, class, and respect. Stay focused on what's important: your children. Don't start speaking ill of this new person. This only serves to make it more difficult for you and the children to positively move forward. Save the "Can you *believe* it!?" speech for when you and your friends are out for an adult beverage. The only issues that should be in the forefront are how this new individual treats your children, and making that relationship transition as easy as possible for your kids.

Be Powerful

When the time comes for your ex to bring their new significant other into your child's life, it can be a large and bitter pill to swallow. Let me set up a few examples of what you might be feeling...*and* how to handle it.

You might be feeling...

Replaced: Your ex has found a new partner and that person is replacing you, taking your spot in what used to be "your world."

Fearful: You're frightened of the unknown, and of how the new partner will treat you and your children.

Jealous: You feel that your ex has "beaten you" by finding someone first, while you continue to search for Mr./Mrs. Right.

Insecure: You're having irrational thoughts of your child liking the new partner better than you.

These are all common emotions that many experience during the introduction of a new partner. As overwhelming and real as you may believe these to be, the truth is that these are all irrational fears. They will not come true unless you allow them to be true.

No one is replacing you. *You* are irreplaceable! You will always be your child's Mommy or Daddy, no matter how many new partners are in the mix. Keep your mind positive. You are what you think you are, so think strong thoughts! Dwell in the negative and that's what you'll get.

Fear not; you are strong and confident. You will give respect in order to have it reciprocated. You are the shining example of who you want your child to be. Remember, people treat you the way you allow them to treat you.

Jealousy and resentment will make you sick and less effective as a person and as a parent. Your time will come. It's better to put that energy into meeting someone worthy of you as opposed to envying someone else's life. Don't be jealous; no human who walks this earth has a life of bliss.

Don't be insecure; take control and visualize what type of positive relationship you want with your ex's new partner. You don't have to be friends; you just need to find common ground for the sake of the children. Exhibiting confidence and maturity will teach your children a very valuable life lesson. Take control of your own destiny; do not allow anyone else to map out your life journey.

. . . .

"If you have no confidence in self, you are twice defeated in the race of life."

—MARCUS GARVEY

. . . .

Ask Questions

Both you and your ex should have the same objectives when it comes to the children—safety, love, and their well-being. When a new partner is put into the mix, it's important to ask questions. You need to know who they are; will your children be safe?

Now, make no mistake: There is a big difference between asking relevant questions and being just plain difficult and combative. This is not about you and your ex. This is about the well-being of your children. All you need to know at this time is, are they walking around with an ankle bracelet or standing on a 12-page rap sheet? Ask questions and be informed.

. . . .

> *"A child who is allowed to be*
> *disrespectful to his parents*
> *will not have true respect*
> *for anyone."*
>
> —Billy Graham

. . . .

Set the Example

Your children will always look to you for guidance. You are the one who teaches them to be respectful, appreciative, humble, worthy, kind, giving, loving, and accepting. But you are also the one who teaches them to be angry, jealous, deceitful, cruel, violent, envious, mean, disrespectful, and malicious. Your words and your actions will resonate with your children, and will affect them for years to come. What kind of parent do you wish to be and what kind of people do you wish your children to be?

. . . .

"Everybody knows how to raise children, except the people who have them."

—P. J. O'ROURKE

. . . .

WHEN YOU SAID

"It's not you, it's me."

Did you think those words would make it easier for me to set you free?

"Honey, I love you, but it's just not like before."

Did you think that would make it easier for me to walk out the door?

"Marriage was just not for me."

Did you think I'd have doubted your honesty?

When you said "I do" those years before

Did you never think that you needed more?

When you said my touch leaves you cold all through

Did you think I did not know there was someone new?

"I think our child has your beautiful blue eyes."

Why would I ever expect your goodbyes?

BOUNDARIES!

Setting boundaries in divorce is extremely important for all parties involved. By setting boundaries, you provide yourself and your children the physical and emotional space needed for a productive and sound family unit.

It is in everyone's best interest to set boundaries early on and remain consistent and firm. A good way to begin is by setting up a parenting plan—a list of topics and issues that you and your ex can agree upon for discussion. Eliminating topics that are not appropriate and are not acceptable for conversation will help establish a peaceful co-existence in the world of dual parenting.

When boundaries are *not* put into place, the risks of encountering complicated and increasingly combative scenarios becomes much greater. Lines will be crossed, feelings will be hurt, and your children will undoubtedly be the ones caught painfully in the middle.

So, leave nothing to chance and set up the boundaries you need sooner, rather than later.

Communication Boundaries

Make your calling times age-appropriate. No one wants their ex calling to chat with the kids at 11:00 P.M. on a school night; it's not appropriate and it is abusive to put your child in a situation that could hurt his or her performance in class the next day.

When your ex is with the children, limit how often you communicate with them. When enjoying a nice visitation weekend with the kids, no one needs the ex calling in every two hours to "assess the situation." Only communicate and entertain issues that are directly related to your children.

Take the high road when communicating with your ex. There is no need for derogatory remarks and foul language; try to keep things amicable and respectful. Your children will thank you for it.

. . . .

*"Boundaries are to protect
life, not to limit pleasures."*

—EDWIN LOUIS COLE

. . . .

Personal Boundaries

You and your ex need to stay out of each other's lives. You don't need to know where the other goes, what they do, what they think, or whom they are seeing. Keep personal space and boundaries in focus.

Keep your conversations generic and to the point. Your ex is just that, your *ex*. There is no need to discuss your fears, concerns, or personal issues with them. Don't talk about anything that might open the door to confusion or emotional entanglements. Keep the conversations directly related to your children.

If you're feeling "used" or "taken advantage of," chances are you have not set up sufficient personal boundaries. It's okay to say, "No" or, "I'm sorry, I will not be doing that." These few simple words can be your key to emotional freedom.

. . . .

"Daring to set boundaries is about having the courage to love ourselves, even when we risk disappointing others."

—BRENE BROWN

. . . .

Family Boundaries

Family house rules should be consistent, regardless of whose house the children are visiting. Some examples are bed times, dietary needs, and respect for any new spouses that come along.

Punishments and rewards should also be consistent in both homes.

Confirm and keep to drop-off and pick-up schedules and visitation days. Make it a point to stick to the days and times that were established in your divorce agreement. Exceptions can only be made if both parties approve of the changes.

Do not involve the children in your adult communications, regardless of how benign you think they may be.

. . . .

> *"If your boundary training
> consists only of words, you
> are wasting your breath. But
> if you 'do' boundaries with
> your kids, they internalize
> the experiences, remember
> them, digest them, and make
> them part of how they see
> reality."*
>
> —HENRY CLOUD

. . . .

Communicate Clearly

Say what you mean and mean what you say. When setting boundaries, there should be no gray areas; no "what ifs" and no manipulating terms. Boundaries should be set to protect you, your ex, and your children. Doing this will alleviate many unforeseen toxic conflicts. Boundaries should be fair, consistent, and respectful. Communicate early and firmly what is (and is not) negotiable. This does not mean to be confrontational or arrogant. It's time to listen and respect each other's limitations.

. . . .

> *"First learn the meaning*
> *of what you say, and then*
> *speak."*
>
> —EPICTETUS

. . . .

Don't Take It Personally

If you're looking for peaceful co-existence in the world of dual parenting, boundaries are a crucial necessity.

Some of you may look at boundaries as a personal attack against you. You feel suffocated by the idea of having restrictions and limitations on issues when at one time you were the master of ceremonies. It's time to check your ego at the door and stop wasting your energy on trying to be the band leader. Hop on board the train of collaboration—and *stay* awhile.

Remember that your number one goal should be to provide you and your children with a peaceful, calm, and positive co-existence with your ex. The way you will reach that goal is by setting, supporting, and standing firm with your boundaries.

. . . .

*"And this is one of the major
questions of our lives: how
we keep boundaries, what
permission we have to cross
boundaries, and how we
do so."*

—A. B. YEHOSHUA

. . . .

BOUNDARIES

Boundaries are here to help us thrive.

They are not here to punish or deprive.

You may be angry, hurt, and confused,

But these boundaries protect us from
being abused.

There need to be limits, restrictions,
and space,

As having them will keep us all in a
good place.

So when you start venting about
your day

Don't be upset if I just walk away.

TEENS CRY, TOO

Divorced parents of teens, this one's for you.

Many times, teens are a forgotten victim during this difficult transition. Unlike the younger child of divorce, the teenager already has a lot of family memories in their personal archives. But their personal sense of loss, abandonment, and anger can be overwhelming, and communicating it to you can be even more of a challenge. It's been well documented that the average teenager barely converses with their parents when there are no issues at hand, so trying to read them during a stressful period like divorce can feel nearly impossible.

Chances are that your teens will not be the ones initiating the dialogue; it will be your responsibility to launch that ship of conversation. Remember: Keeping your avenues of communication open is crucial. You must be ready and willing to listen *and* validate what they are saying, even if you don't agree. Though their words and thoughts may differ from your agenda, this is not the time for you to read from a manifesto. This is the time to make them feel like you have listened, comprehended, and *respected* what they have articulated.

Don't make this about you. Don't make this a debate. Remember, even though they may *look* like adults, they are *not*. It would be painfully cruel and destructively selfish for you to summon your child into the arena of adulthood prematurely.

Just Listen

Clear your mind of what you *think* your teen feels, and open your ears to hear what *they* believe to be true. This is the moment when your ability to listen should supersede any other of your senses. Sometimes, just know-ing they've been heard can hold the key to one's refuge and sanity. When all else fails, just listen.

. . . .

"One of the most sincere
forms of respect is actually
listening to what another
has to say."

—BRYANT H. MCGILL

. . . .

Be Supportive

What's important to remember is that, when dealing with the topic of divorce, you need to be on a platform separate from that of everyday teen issues.

Be the port in the storm your teen needs. Be empathetic toward their fears and worries. Give them space to vent and communicate concerns without the dread of being ridiculed, questioned, or judged. Now is not the time to lecture. Trust me; you'll have plenty of opportunities with future teen matters to do that.

. . . .

*"Our chief want is someone
who will inspire us to be
what we know we could be."*

—RALPH WALDO EMERSON

. . . .

IF YOU ONLY KNEW HOW I CRY, TOO

If you only knew how I cry, too
I wish I was strong enough to hold you on
my shoulder.
But I need some more time in life to get a
bit older.

I wish I could fix all of your pain,
And bring you both together again.

But my years are not enough, you see,
And knowing that is hard on me.

Please understand, I love the both of you,
So please don't ask of me what I cannot do.
Oh, if you only knew how I cry too.

**YOU CAN'T
UN-RING A BELL**

Be careful of what you say. Your words are powerful weapons, and once they've been launched, they cannot be unspoken.

Many of us have few kind words to speak when it comes to our ex. However, publicly airing your dirty laundry will only come back to haunt you in the end. The private, intimate history you share with your ex is nobody's business. Bashing, belittling, blaming, or blasting your ex might momentarily make you feel better, but the reality is that's a game with no winners.

Your children hear far more than you might think, and get their information from places you least suspect. The last thing you need is to be playing a game of telephone with your children, having them come back to you with gossip heard second-hand about you or your ex. What purpose would this mockery serve? Answer: *none*. It serves no purpose other than publicly embarrassing and humiliating your children.

Choose your words wisely and always take the high road. Once you choose to ring that bell, it cannot be un-rung.

Think Before You Speak

The power that your words hold over your children is so strong that it goes beyond influential. Children pick up on words, tone, and attitude like a sponge soaking up water. So, when speaking of your ex-spouse, keep the dialogue as positive as possible. Remember the motto you learned in kindergarten? "If you have nothing nice to say, say nothing at all." Well, tattoo that on your brain.

Articulating a negative declaration against your ex will only provide your children with the ingredients for a perfect storm of doubt, confusion, and anger, both toward your ex and toward *you*. Children are more willing to accept what they're told at face value. And, if what you're telling them goes against what they feel toward their other parent, they can become confused or frustrated, and may even being to distrust you. Just remember to think before you speak—your words are more commanding than you know.

. . . .

*"Words have special powers
...to lift up or put down...to
heal or harm. Choose your
words carefully."*

—A.D. WILLIAMS

. . . .

Kill Them With Kindness

There's something that you will need to accept unconditionally moving forward: you no longer have any ability to manage what your ex says about you. What you can control, however, is how you choose to respond. The best technique by far is to "kill them with kindness." It's a tactic that those who choose to bad-mouth others rarely see coming and are utterly unprepared to retaliate against.

It's hard to deny the power of a smile and a kind response when it's injected into an unstable dialogue. And the fact is that it's impossible to keep a fire going without any fuel. Keep peace in your heart, and keep calm in your head.

. . . .

"Too often we underestimate the power of a touch, a smile, a kind word, a listening ear, an honest compliment, or the smallest act of caring, all of which have the potential to turn a life around."

—LEO BUSCAGLIA

. . . .

YOU CAN'T UN-RING A BELL

I am sad for the person you've become
The lies and the rumors cannot be undone
You stand on your soapbox and preach
  to the lot
As if to convince them you're great and
  I'm not
At first I was hurt, and embarrassed,
  and mad
But now that I'm free of you I am just
  glad.
My advice is just this, and you'd best
  mark it well:
No one—but no one—can unring a bell.

WOULD YOU RATHER BE HAPPY OR RIGHT?

Choosing between being happy and being right is easier said than done; it takes a lot of practice. Nobody wants to be wrong or on the losing end of an argument—especially with your ex!

But there comes a time in your life when you just need to grow up and realize how little it matters. After a while, you can become so obsessed with being the victor that you lose sight of just what you were discussing and debating in the first place. When you begin losing sight of the subject of your disagreement, you start going through your mental Rolodex, spewing out old ammunition to prove you're "right," so that you can "win."

News flash—by doing that, you've just lost. Stop wasting your time and energy trying to make someone agree with you, or trying to make them understand that what you believe is right.

No matter how hard you try, you cannot fit a square peg in a round hole. There comes a time when you just need to let go and move on. Agree to disagree; you will be a happier person in the long run and your children will thank you.

Pick and Choose Your Battles

There will always be difficult people in your life who have the overwhelming need to be right. It doesn't matter if they're talking about the weather, a movie, or a football game. They will always stretch the truth to fit their version, so as to come out victorious. And this only becomes less tolerable when the nonsense is coming straight from your ex's mouth.

If your ex is stubbornly debating you on an issue that truly holds no bearing on the well-being of your children—if their only intention is to earn the "I'm Right" award—you are well within your rights to practice picking and choosing your battles.

Exhibiting self-control and quickly putting out the little fires that threaten to flare up into a blaze of endless debate will give you peace of mind and power in what would normally be a powerless position. You will be amazed at how quickly the "right-fighter" pulls back when they have no one to debate with. And hopefully one day your "right-fighter" will choose to be happy over being right.

Because some fights are just not worth fighting.

. . . .

"An ounce of practice is worth more than tons of preaching."

—Mahatma Gandhi

. . . .

The Sky Is Green?

You cannot control what other people believe. While you can marvel at the too-blue sky, another's vision could be a sky of green. Don't waste your time and energy on trying to make sense of someone else's distorted take on life. Revel in your own positive vision and never stop drinking in the beauty that surrounds you.

. . . .

"Don't make your life diffi-cult. Life is for you to enjoy so, create your beautiful life using your powerful imagination."

—UNKNOWN

. . . .

OKAY, YOU'RE RIGHT!

We've danced this dance a million times

I've heard all of your usual lines

If things aren't going all your way

You're prone to throw it all away

It's such a drain to dance your tune

As slowly I become immune

To all your pleas and protestations

Which now inspire deep frustrations

I've grown so tired of this fight.

That's it. You win. I'm sorry. You're RIGHT.

FINAL WORD

·····················

As you prepare to close this little book, I hope you are departing with a healthier and more positive view on how to be a better parent to your child, and a less combative adult to your ex.

When all else fails, just remember:

You need to *LOVE* your child more than you *HATE* your ex!

ABOUT HELEN FRIED

Remarried in 2006, Helen Fried found the intricacies of dealing with a blended family and ex-spouses to be quite trying. She founded a monthly support group to allow others with similar divorce stories to vent, working together to grow from their hardships. Residing in Weston, Florida, Fried continues to write as she works to build a happy family with her husband Steve Fried, children Nicolas and Lexi, and step-children Matthew and Danielle.